THE BEST
CONCERTINA METHOD
YET

By BOB KAIL

The Concertina is a folk instrument --- a simple instrument---fun to play, part of our heritage from Ireland and England and Italy. Concertina music is so ingrained, so natural a sound that you know it's authentic at the first echo of the Civil War and Nineteenth Century airs that fill up the treasure chest of this book.

Concertinas are great for the popular music of today. You can accompany, play a melody, or sing along as you lead your friends in the song you learn without a teacher by following the easy a guide-lines of this book.

Our company is proud to add this volume to our BEST-YET methods for easy instruments because we think it will bring even more thousands of happy players to join the throngs already having FUN WITH MUSIC.

R. K.
Ashley Publications
Carlstadt, New Jersey

ELEMENTARY MUSIC PRINCIPLES

You don't have to read music to play the concertina but certain elementary principles may be helpful. For example:

Music is divided into TIME UNITS (measures) pictured on a STAFF (5 lines and 4 spaces) on which music notes are placed.

The illustration to the right is a STAFF. It opens with a CLEF sign. The vertical lines divide the staff into measures to impart regularity to the music.

Notes go through the lines or in the spaces. Some notes are below or above the limited compass of the Staff. Such notes are expressed by short lines added below or above the staff, called ledger lines.

These are MUSIC NOTES

Whole note (4 beats): 𝗼

Half note (2 beats):

Quarter note (1 beat):

Eighth note (2 to a beat):

Connected 8th notes:

(We use "quarter notes" in illustrations

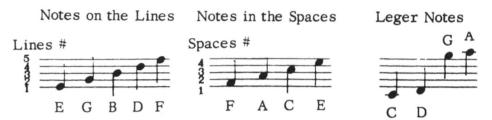

Notes on the Lines — Lines # — E G B D F

Notes in the Spaces — Spaces # — F A C E

Leger Notes — G A / C D

Note the alphabetic sequence when we put these all together:

C D E F G A B C D E F G A

Notes illustrated are WHOLE TONES which can be lowered or raised to the next half-tone by means of FLATS (♭) to lower a tone and SHARPS (♯) to raise a tone. A sign like this (♮) is called a NATURAL, which restores a flatted or sharped note to its basic tone.

The presence of one or more FLATS or SHARPS after the clef sign means that every such note in the piece is flatted or sharped. For instance, a flat on the middle line (B) means that every B becomes B♭, a sharp on the top line (F) means that every F becomes F♯.

Before each piece of music, you will see a "TIME SIGNATURE", like $\frac{2}{4}$ $\frac{3}{4}$ $\frac{4}{4}$ or C (same as $\frac{4}{4}$).

$\frac{2}{4}$ time means 2 beats to a measure, a popular tempo for polkas and one-steps. $\frac{3}{4}$ time means 3 beats to a measure, used mainly for waltzes. $\frac{4}{4}$ or C time means 4 beats to a measure, used in most dance music, popular songs and ballads.

A dot after a note increases its value 50%. For instance, a dotted HALF NOTE 𝅗𝅥. takes 3 beats.

Each note has its equivalent in SILENT value, like this: (called "rests")

WHOLE REST   HALF NOTE REST   QUARTER NOTE REST   1/8TH REST

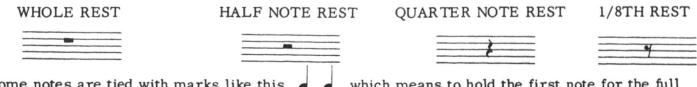

Some notes are tied with marks like this   which means to hold the first note for the full time value of both notes.

THE BEST CONCERTINA METHOD YET

By BOB KAIL

CONTENTS

plus
PULL-OUT FINGERING CHART
and
(with words and music)

and
(for concertina and piano)

The Concertina

---- most often used is the German or Anglo-Saxon instrument with twenty keys. Pull out our pull-out diagram and pick up your concertina.

Put the fingers of each hand through the straps on each side. Thumbs stay outside. Rest your fingers on the keys. Hold down the thumb key. (See it by your right thumb? Check the diagram.) Try a few ins and outs with the bellows...GENTLY. Treat this instrument like a lover and you will make beautiful music together. Don't force it! Don't twist the bellows. Do not draw or press the bellows without playing a key. If you want silence, use the thumb key.

Are the hand straps loose enough to let your fingers move freely from key to key? Are they tight enough so that you won't drop the instrument on your toes? If your concertina seems too heavy, rig up a saxophone strap around your neck to help hold the weight.

Concertina Notation System

D means draw the bellows out, causing air to enter through any depressed reeds and making a musical sound. P means to Press the concertina together --- expelling air and thus making the reeds vibrate if any keys are being pressed.

On this, the usual type of concertina, each key opened will play one note when the bellows are pressed and a different note when the bellows are drawn out . . . like a harmonica. Each key is numbered: one through ten is for the right hand, 1. through 10. is for the left hand.

Scales

Here are the scales most often used on the concertina. You can play them now or turn the page and return to them later.

Scale of C major.
(All naturals.)

Scale of G major.
(One sharp.)

Exercises
For the Concertina

Right Hand.

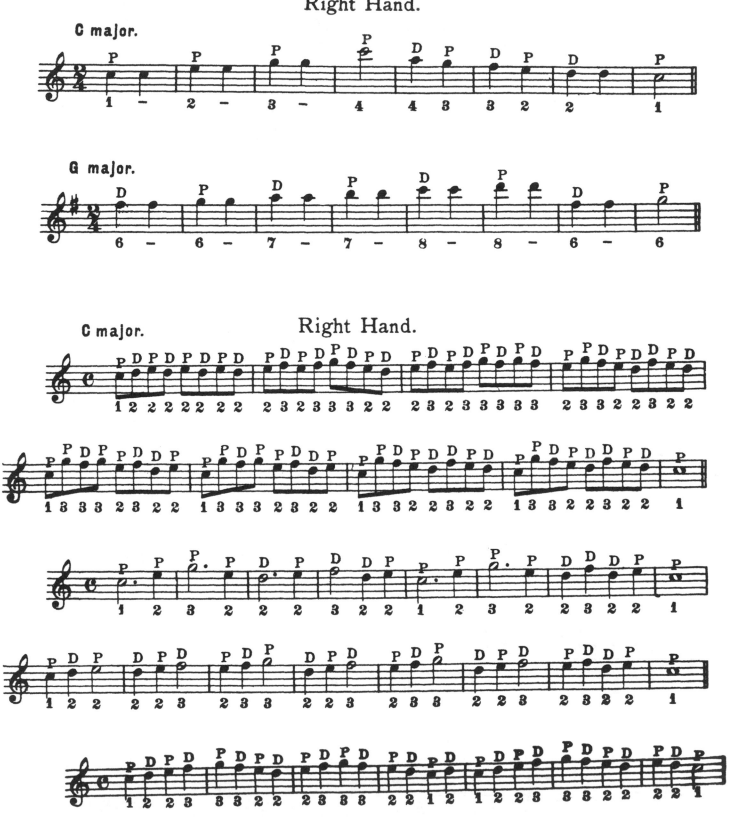

6

Lord Lovell.

Sparking Sunday Night.

Strike the Cymbal.

Cracovienne.

Indian Death Song.

CIELITO LINDO
(BEAUTIFUL HEAVEN)

CARLOS FERNANDEZ

Moderate waltz

CHORUS (Spanish vocal)

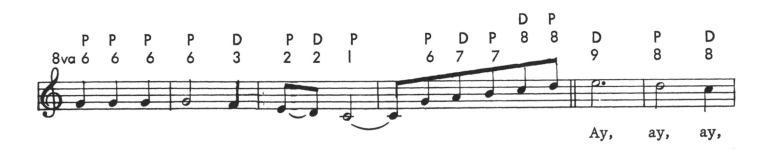

Ay, ay, ay,

ay! _____ Can - ta y no llo - res, _____ Por - que can-tan-do se a

le - gran Cie - li - to Lin - do los co - ra - zo - nes. _____

THE MARINES' HYMN

U. S. MARINE CORPS SONG

Right Hand Only
(Plays 8 notes higher)

WHEN THE SAINTS GO MARCHING IN

Moderate march tempo

FOLK SONG

10

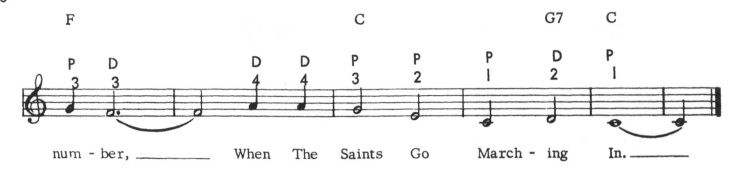

O SUSANNA

STEPHEN FOSTER

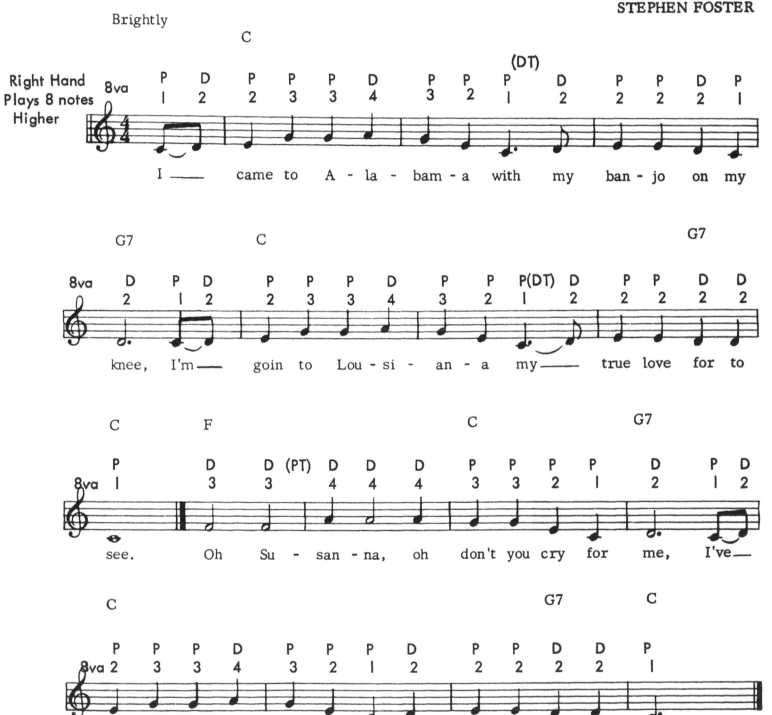

Left Hand.(•)

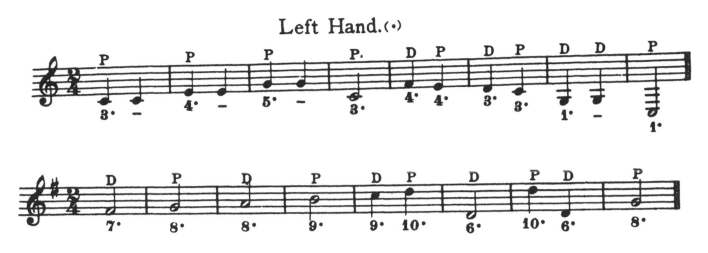

SHENANDOAH

Moderately

FOLK SONG

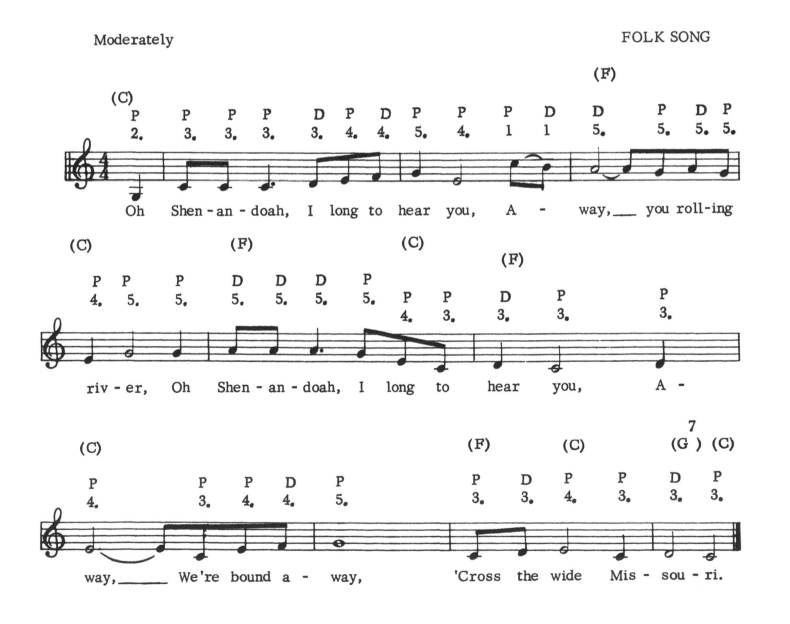

Oh Shen - an - doah, I long to hear you, A - way,___ you roll-ing

riv - er, Oh Shen - an - doah, I long to hear you, A -

way,_____ We're bound a - way, 'Cross the wide Mis - sou - ri.

THE WABASH CANNONBALL

With spirit

Folk Song

(DT)

P	P	P	P	P	D	P	P	P	P	P	P	D	P	D	D	D
5.	5.	5.	5.	1	2	2	3	3	3	2	2	1	4.	5.	5.	

From the great At - lan - tic O - cean to the wide Pa - cif - ic shore, From the

P	P	D	D	P	D	P	P	D	D	D	D	P	P	P	P	P	D
5.	5.	1	2	2	2	1	1	1	1	1	5.		5.	5.	5.	1	2

queen of flow-ing moun-tains to the south - land by the shore, She's might-y tall and

P	P			P	P	P	D	P	D		D	D	P	P	D	D	P	D	D	P
2	3		2	2	2	2	1	4.		5.	5.	5.	5.	1	2	2	2	2 1

hand-some and quite well known by all. Ev-'ry - bod - y loves the choo choo of the

D	P	D	D		P		P	P	P	D	P	3	2	P	P	D	P
1	5,	5.	1	1		5.	5.	1	2	2				2	2	2	1

Wa - bash Can - non - ball. Lis - ten to the jin - gle, The rum-ble and the

D		P	P	D	D	P	D	D	D	D	P	D	D	P		P	P
4.		5.	5.	1	2	2	2	2	2	1	1	1	5.	5.		5.	5.

roar, Glid - ing thru the wood-lands thru the hills and by the shore. Hear the

P	P	P	D	P	P	P	P	P	P	D	P	D
5.	5.	1	2	2	3	3	3	2	2	2	1	4

mu - sic of the en - gine which was nev - er known to stall,

P	P	D	D	P	D	D	D	D	P	D	D	P
5.	5.	1	2	2	2	2	2	1	5.	5.	1	1

Trav-'ling thru the jun - gles, Goes the Wa - bash Can - non - ball.

CARELESS LOVE

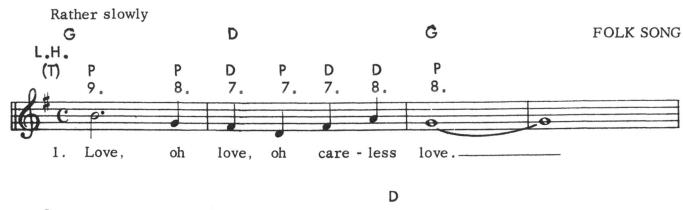

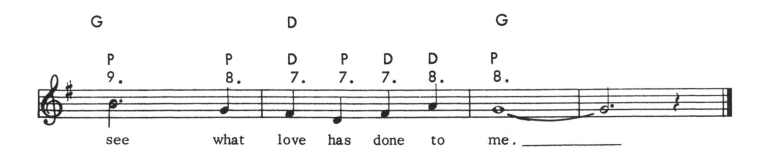

2. I was happy as can be,
   Days were sunny and so free,
   You came along and done me wrong,
   You brought a careless love to me.

3. Oh! the anguish in my heart,
   Oh! the anguish in my heart,
   Your love was just a careless love,
   A love from which we had to part.

****

THE BLUE TAIL FLY

TRADITIONAL

Lively

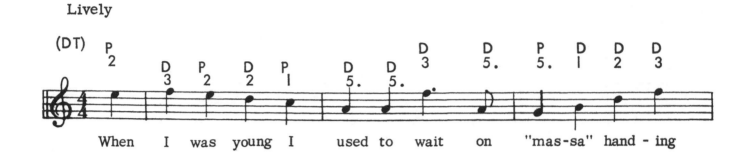

When I was young I used to wait on "mas-sa" hand - ing

him his plate, And pass the bot-tle when he got dry, And

brush a - way the blue tail fly. Jim - mie crack corn and

I don't care, Jim - mie crack corn and I don't care,

Jim-mie crack corn and I don't care, My mas - ter's gone a - way!

BATTLE HYMN OF THE REPUBLIC

Home, Sweet Home.

Augusta's Favorite.

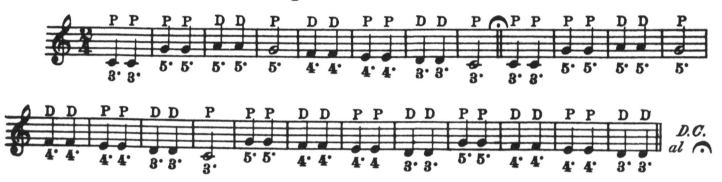

Twilight Dews.

Charley Over the Water.

Left and Right Hand.

Listen to the Nightingale.

Comin' Thro' the Rye.

Bryan O'Lynn.

No, Ne'er Can Thy Home Be Mine.

The Coquette.

MY WILD IRISH ROSE

Moderate waltz tempo

CHAUNCEY OLCOTT

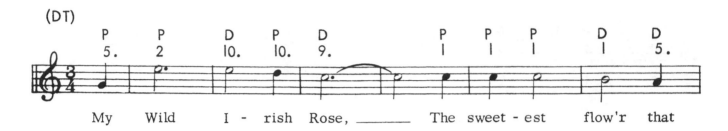

My Wild I - rish Rose, _____ The sweet - est flow'r that

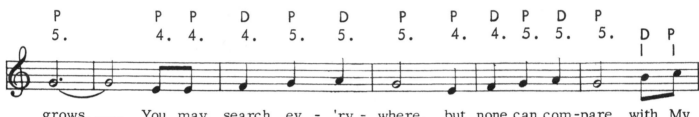

grows, ___ You may search ev - 'ry - where, but none can com-pare with My

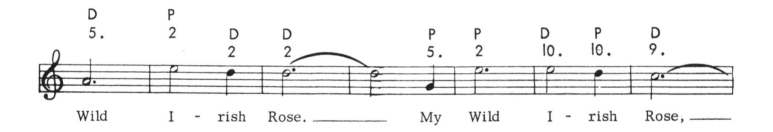

Wild I - rish Rose. _____ My Wild I - rish Rose, _____

___ The dear - est flow'r that grows, _____ And some day for my

sake, she may let me take the bloom from My Wild I - rish Rose. _____

LITTLE BROWN JUG

FOLK SONG

Rather fast

My wife and I live all a - lone, In a

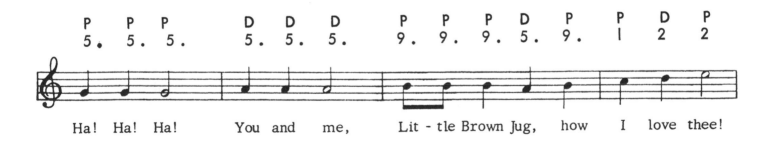

lit - tle log hut we call our own. She loves gin and

I love rum, I tell you we have lots of fun.

Ha! Ha! Ha! You and me, Lit - tle Brown Jug, how I love thee!

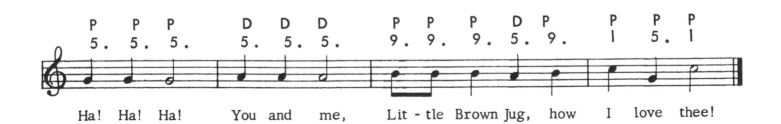

Ha! Ha! Ha! You and me, Lit - tle Brown Jug, how I love thee!

SCARBOROUGH FAIR

Rather slowly

Adaptation by ALBERT GAMSE

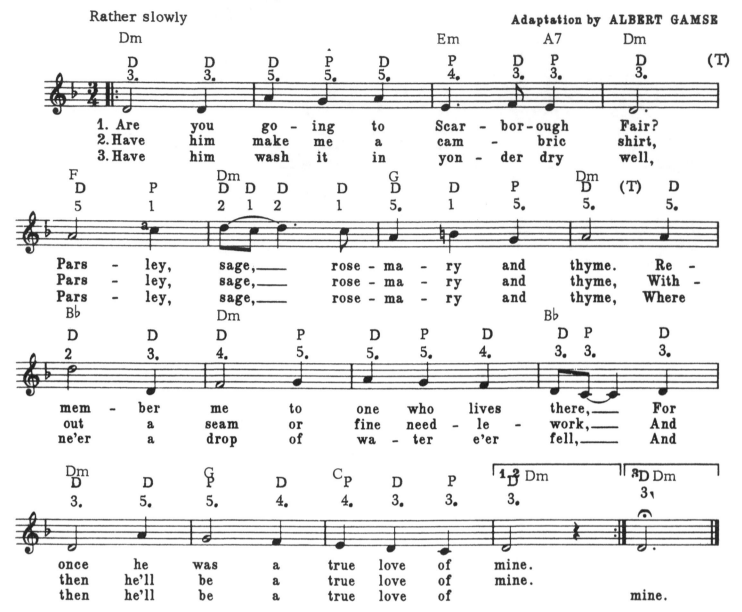

1. Are you go - ing to Scar - bor - ough Fair?
2. Have him make me a cam - bric shirt,
3. Have him wash it in yon - der dry well,

Pars - ley, sage,____ rose - ma - ry and thyme. Re -
Pars - ley, sage,____ rose - ma - ry and thyme, With -
Pars - ley, sage,____ rose - ma - ry and thyme, Where

mem - ber me to one who lives there,____ For
out a seam or fine need - le - work,____ And
ne'er a drop of wa - ter e'er fell,____ And

once he was a true love of mine.
then he'll be a true love of mine.
then he'll be a true love of mine.

4. Have him find me an acre of land,
   Parsley, sage, rosemary and thyme,
   Between the sea and over the sand,
   And then he'll be a true love of mine.

5. Plow the land with the horn of a lamb,
   Parsley, sage, rosemary and thyme,
   Then sow some seeds from north of the dam,
   And then he'll be a true love of mine.

6. If he tells me he can't, I'll reply:
   "Parsley, sage, rosemary and thyme"
   Let me know that at least he will try,
   And then he'll be a true love of mine.

7. Love imposes impossible tasks,
   Parsley, sage, rosemary and thyme,
   Though not more than any heart asks,
   And I must know he's a true love of mine.

8. Dear, when thou hast finished thy task,
   Parsley, sage, rosemary and thyme,
   Come to me, my hand for to ask,
   For thou then art a true love of mine.

I LOVE YOU TRULY

Moderately

CARRIE JACOBS BOND

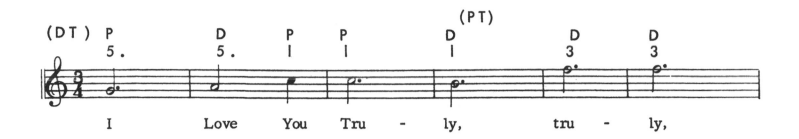

I Love You Tru - ly, tru - ly,

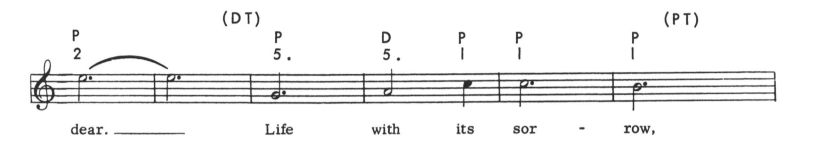

dear. _____ Life with its sor - row,

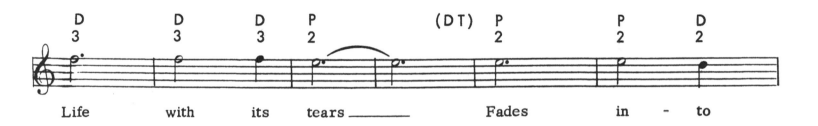

Life with its tears _____ Fades in - to

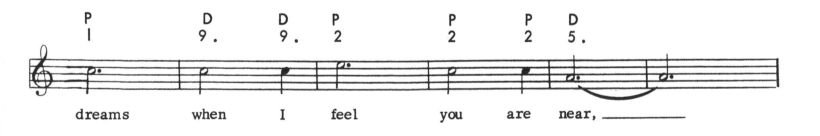

dreams when I feel you are near, _____

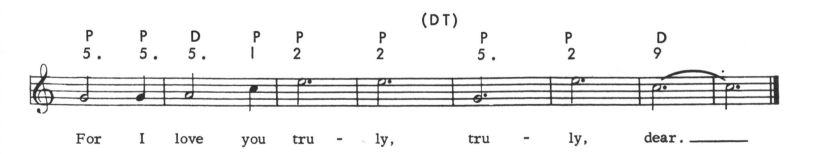

For I love you tru - ly, tru - ly, dear. _____

SILENT NIGHT

Moderately

MOHR - GRUBER

I Heard the Wee Bird Singing.

Old Rosin the Bow.

America.

Yankee Doodle.

Star-Spangled Banner.

The Stars and Stripes For Ever.

Hail, Columbia.

Maryland, My Maryland.

Dixie.

Bonnie Blue Flag.

The Flag of Our Union.

Robin Adair.

Bonnie Dundee.

Camptown Hornpipe.

Ricket's Hornpipe.

Flora's Birthday.

Old Folks at Home.

Massa's in the Cold, Cold Ground.

Marching Thro' Georgia.

My Old Kentucky Home.

We Wont Go Home Till Morning.

Johnny Sands.

Brian Boru.

Nobody Going to Marry Me?

Charming Young Widow.

As I'd Nothing Else to Do.

If I Had But a Thousand a Year.

Ten Little Dancers.

The Bell Goes A-ringing for Sai-rah.

Little Maggie May.

Pulling Hard Against the Stream.

Beautiful Nell.

The Merriest Girl That's Out.

The Harp That Once Thro' Tara's Halls.

John Anderson, My Joe.

Norah, the Pride of Kildare.

Molly Bawn.

Pirates Chorus or "Ever Be Happy."

When Johnnie Comes Marching Home.

Bachelor's Hall.

69.

Lament of the Irish Emigrant.

Keemo Kimo.

The Old Arm-Chair.

Kitty of Coleraine.

Castles in the Air.

What's a' the Steer, Kimmer.

The Bright, Rosy Morning.

In Happy Moments.

From the Opera "Maritana."

Morella's Lesson.

Be Gone, Dull Care.

Bonny Doon.

Glory Hallelujah.

Raw Recruits, or Abraham's Daughter.

Marching Along.

Mary of Argyle.

I'm Leaving Thee in Sorrow, Annie.

Ever of Thee.

Oh, Hear Me, Norma.

Blue Bells of Scotland.

Oh! I Should Like to Marry.

Last Rose of Summer.

The Girl I Left Behind Me.

Maiden's Prayer.

Belle Brandon.

Am I Not Fondly Thine Own.

Jerusalem the Golden.

Do They Think of Me at Home?

Listen to the Mocking Bird.

The Heart That Feels No Sorrow.

Beautiful Belle.

Kildoughalt Fair.

Irish Air.

Widow Machree.

Irish Air.

Teddy, You-Gander, or Bully For You.

Irish Air.

The Low-Backed Car, or The Jolly Ploughman.

Irish Air.

Larry O'Gaff.

Irish Air.

Moll Roon.

Irish Air.

A Life on the Ocean Wave.

Shule Aroon.

Irish Air.

42

Soldier Laddie, or Independence Day.

Pas Styrien.

Maid of Judah, or Silver Moon.

Over the Summer Sea.

"Rigoletto!"

I'd Offer You This Hand of Mine.

Sweet Afton.

Annie Laurie.

Scotch Air.

Sweet Memories of Thee.

44

It Is Better to Laugh Than Be Sighing.

Mountain Maid's Invitation.
Tyrolese Air.

Matrimonial Sweets.

Swiss Boy.

In the Lonely Grove.
"Linda."

O Haste, Crimson Morn.

"Lucia di Lammermoor."

Favorite Song.

"Lucia di Lammermoor."

Come, Come, Soldiers, Come.

Auld Lang Syne.

Dearest Spot on Earth to Me Is Home.

O, Lassie, Art Thou Sleeping Yet?

Her Bright Smile Haunts Me Still.

Lucia March.

"Lucia di Lammermoor."

Pop Goes the Weasel.

How Can I Leave Thee?

Within a Mile of Edinboro' Town.

Sally, Come Up.

I've Nothing Else to Do.

Shabby Genteel.

Chorus.

Kathleen Mavourneen.

Land of Sweet Erin.

Rory O' More.

Kate Kearney.

Chorus Jig.

Irish Washerwoman.

The Tempest.

D.S.

Jordan Am a Hard Road.

Old Zip Coon.

College Hornpipe.

Hunting the Hare, or The Calais Packet.

Chinese Dance. "Hark, the Merry Bells" from "Stradella".

Hail to the Chief.

The Witches' Dance.

Paganini.

Drunken Sailor, or The Monkey's Wedding.

Spanish Dance.

Fred. Wilson's Clog Dance № 1.

Clog Dance № 2.

On the Road to Boston.

Jefferson and Liberty.

Arkansas Traveler.

Haste to the Wedding.

Hob or Knob, or The Campbell's Are Coming.

Money Musk.

Tempest Quickstep.

Grand March in Norma.

55

Scotch March.

Louisville March.

Washington March.

Zouave Quickstep.

Chinese March.

Coronation March.

"Prophet."

Garibaldi March.

Columbian Grand March.

St. Louis Quickstep.

O, Nanny, Wilt Thou Gang With Me.

Jim Crow Polka.

Fine.

D.C.

Helter, Skelter, or Over Sticks and Stones Galop.

Gallopade Quadrille.

Hünten.

Virginia Quickstep.

Gabriella Polka.

Gay and Happy.

Air from Lucia di Lammermoor.

Mabel Waltzes.

Immortellen Waltz.

The Peri Waltz.

Roses Waltz.

Spanish Waltz.

On the Beautiful Blue Danube Waltz.

Dream of the Ocean Waltz.

Il Bacio Waltz.

The Kiss.

Fairy Waltz.

Boston Hop Waltz.

Prima Donna Waltz.

Cinderella Waltz.

Elfin Waltz.

Rochester Schottische.

Diamond Schottische.

Flying Cloud Schottische.

Lancers - Quadrilles.

Nº 1. La Dorset.

Nº 2. Lodoiska.

No. 3. La Native.

No. 4. Les Graces.

No. 5. Les Lancers.

Sacred Melodies.

Old Hundred.

Hebron.

Peterborough.

Zion.

Windham.

Balerma.

Russian National Hymn.

Sicilian Hymn.

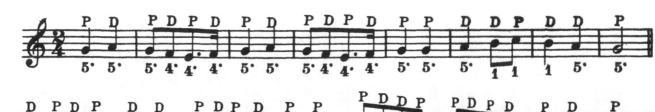

Come, Good Shepherd.

Moulton.

Dover.

St. Thomas.

Golden Hill.

Wilmot.

Cambridge.

Colchester.

Effingham.

Hamburg.

Anvern.

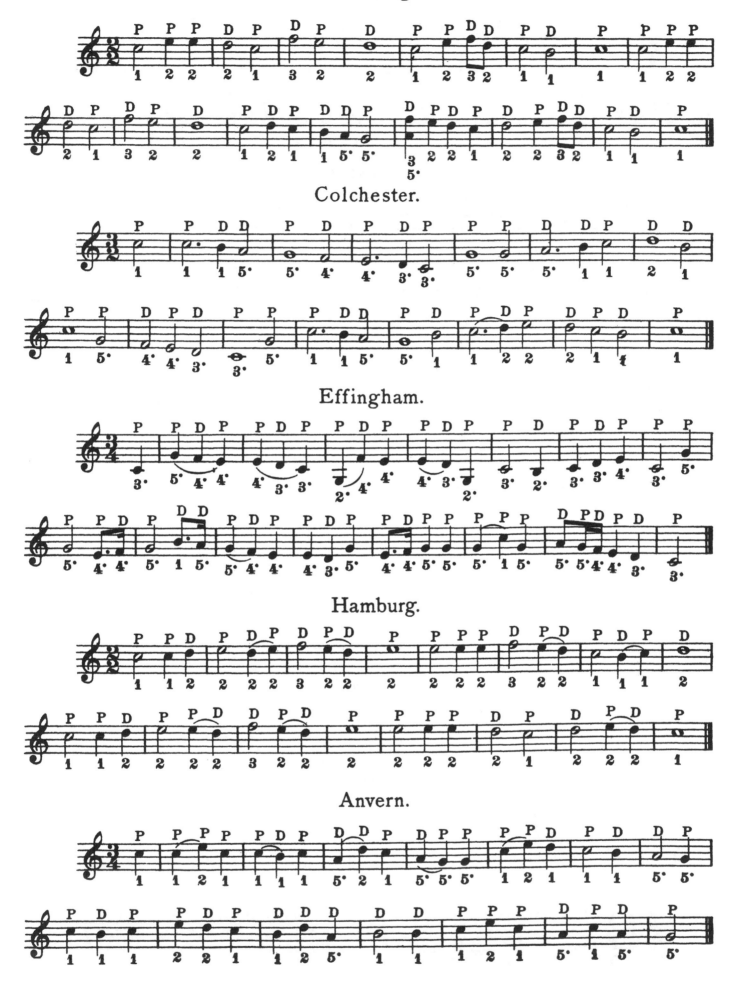

Conway.

Ortonville.

Nichols.

St. Martin's.

Martyrdom.

Clarance.

Hervey.

Mendon.

Cephas.

Jordan.

Land of Rest.

Saw Ye My Saviour.

Dallas.

Alps.

Benevento.

Bower of Prayer.

Dedham.

Troas.

The Morning Light Is Breaking.

Lischer.

Come Ye Disconsulate.

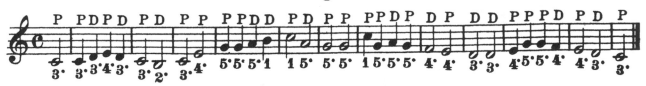

Uxbridge.

Woodstock.

Federal Street.

Prescott.

Oliphant.

Duke Street.

Italian Hymn.

Clifford.

Be Joyful in God, All Ye Lands of the Earth.

How Beauteous Are Their Feet.

Millenium Dawn.

The Lord Is Our Shepherd.

Greenville.

Canaan.

Lisbon.

Oh! How Happy Are They.

Missionary Hymn.

Nashville.

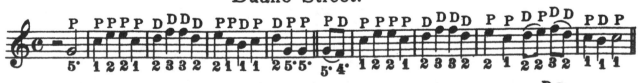

Lanesboro'.

Duane Street.

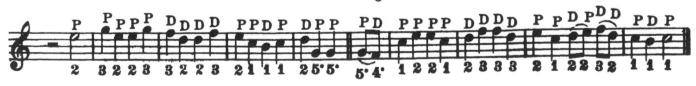

78

My Bible Leads to Glory.

Peace, Troubled Soul.

Rock of Ages.

Nearer, My God, to Thee.

Sweet Bye and Bye.

There Is a Fountain.

I Need Thee Every Hour.

Adeste Fideles.

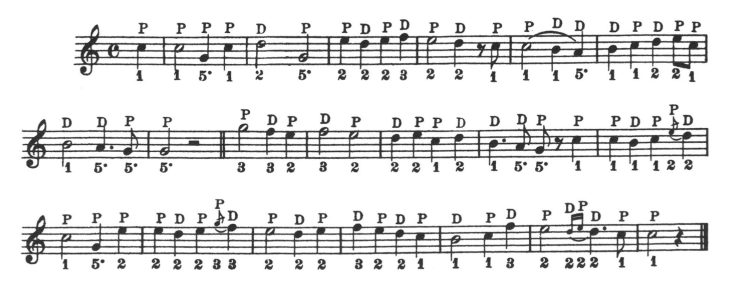

SHE'LL BE COMIN' 'ROUND THE MOUNTAIN

Quite fast, with spirit

FOLK SONG

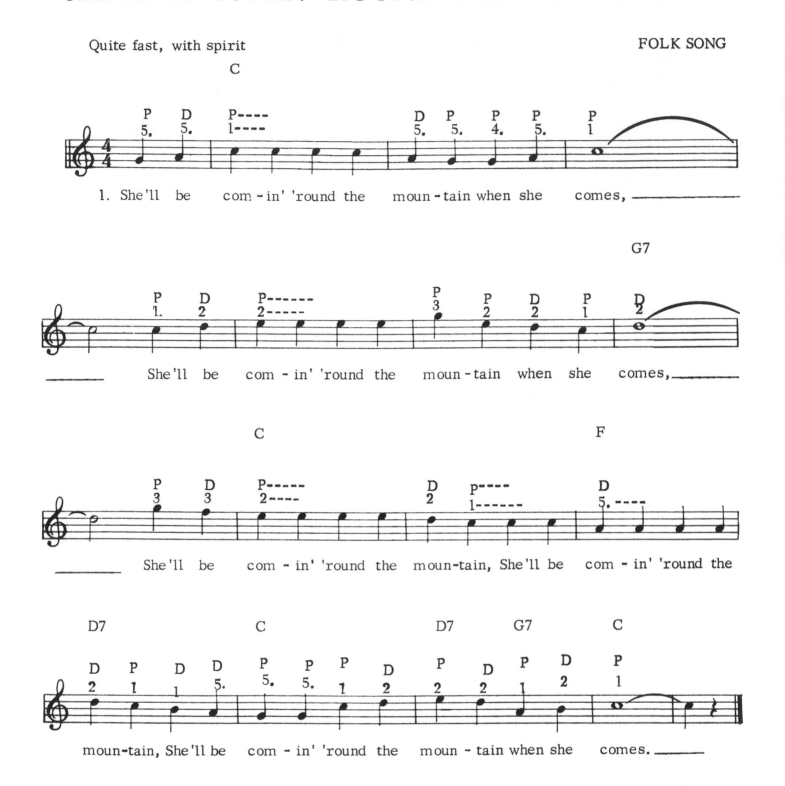

1. She'll be com-in' 'round the moun-tain when she comes,_____ _____ She'll be com-in' 'round the moun-tain when she comes,_____ _____ She'll be com-in' 'round the moun-tain, She'll be com-in' 'round the moun-tain, She'll be com-in' 'round the moun-tain when she comes. _____

2. She'll be driving six white horses when she comes.   (Repeat as above)

3. We will all go out to meet her when she comes.   (Repeat as above)

4. She'll be puffin' and a-steamin' when she comes.   (Repeat as above)

5. She'll be comin' 'round the mountain when she comes.   (Repeat as above)

THE MAN ON THE FLYING TRAPEZE

Moderate waltz

TRADITIONAL

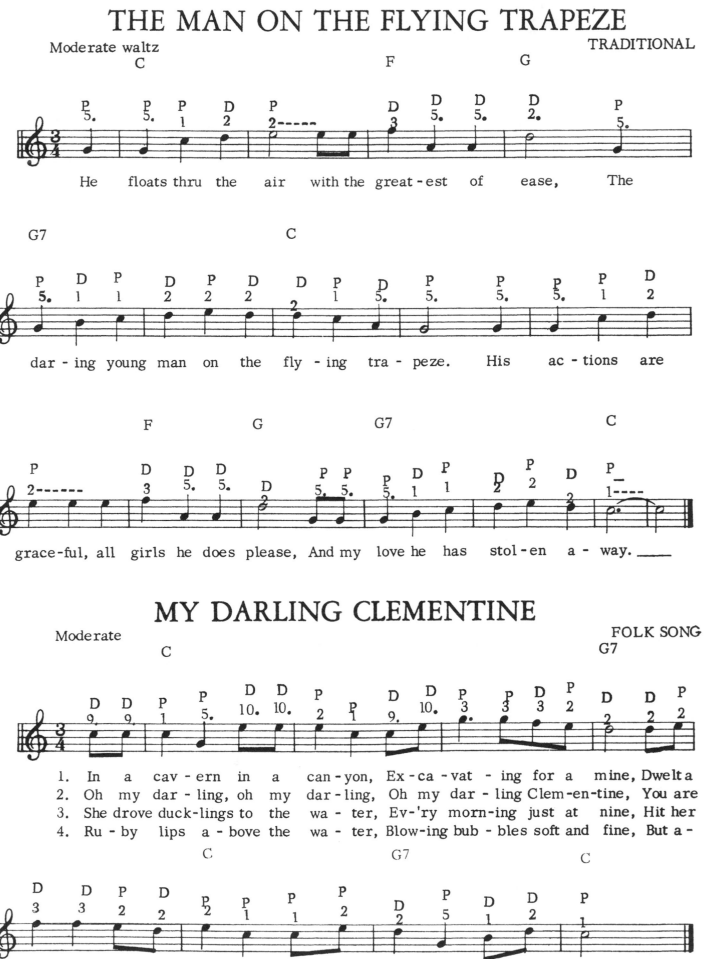

He floats thru the air with the great-est of ease, The dar-ing young man on the fly-ing tra-peze. His ac-tions are grace-ful, all girls he does please, And my love he has stol-en a - way.____

MY DARLING CLEMENTINE

Moderate

FOLK SONG

1. In a cav-ern in a can-yon, Ex-ca-vat-ing for a mine, Dwelt a
2. Oh my dar-ling, oh my dar-ling, Oh my dar-ling Clem-en-tine, You are
3. She drove duck-lings to the wa-ter, Ev-'ry morn-ing just at nine, Hit her
4. Ru - by lips a-bove the wa-ter, Blow-ing bub-bles soft and fine, But a-

min - er, For-ty nin - er, And his daugh-ter, Clem-en - tine.
lost and gone for-ev - er, Dread-ful sor - ry, Clem-en - tine.
big toe 'gainst a splint-er, Fell in - to the foam-ing brine.
las! I was no swim-mer, So I lost my Clem-en - tine. (Repeat #2)

THE ENTERTAINER

A BICYCLE BUILT FOR TWO

Bright waltz tempo

HARRY DACRE

ON TOP OF OLD SMOKY

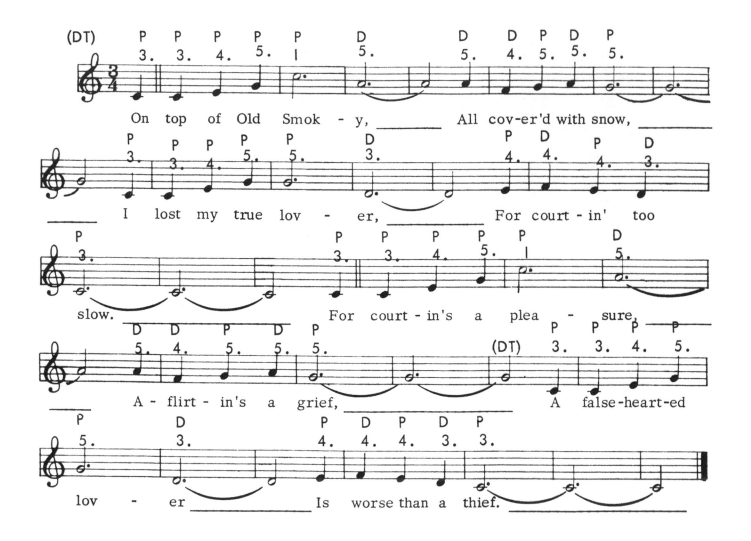

THE CAMPTOWN RACES

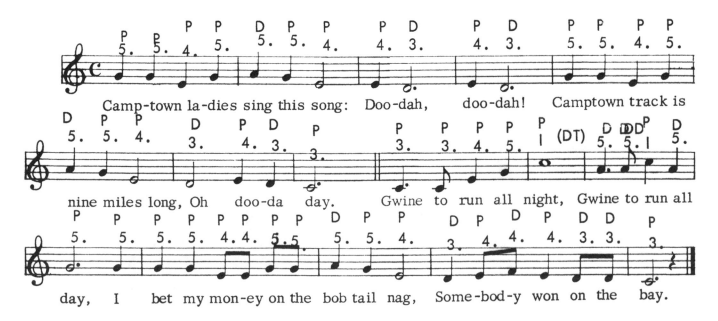

IN THE GOOD OLD SUMMER TIME

RAY SHIELDS
GEORGE EVANS

In the good old sum-mer time, _____ In the good old

sum-mer time, _____ Stroll-ing through the sha-dy lanes

with your "ba - by mine", _____ You hold her hand and

she holds yours and that's a ve-ry good sign _____ That she's your

toot-sie woot-sie in the good old sum-mer time. _____

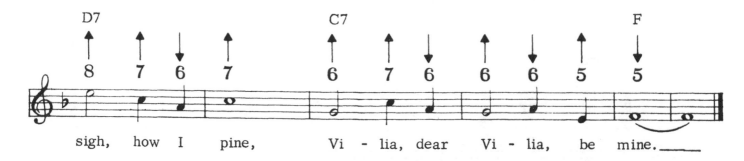

sigh, how I pine, Vi - lia, dear Vi - lia, be mine.____

I'VE BEEN WORKING ON THE RAILROAD

FOLK SONG

I've been work-ing on the rail - road, All the live - long day.

I've been work-ing on the rail - road, To pass the time a - way.

Don't you hear the whis-tle blow - ing? Rise up ear-ly in the morn,

Don't you hear the Cap-tain shout - ing: "Oh Di - nah blow your horn!"

Exercises for the Left Hand

In this exercise you should start by silently drawing the bellows (DT), drawing air by using the thumb key. We must often plan ahead so that there will always be enough air to play a long series of P or D notes. Conserve air by playing short notes--- barely touching the keys -- or by playing softly. When necessary, fill the bellows (PT) or silently (DT) between phrases.

Waltz Accompaniment Exercise

(Just touch the keys, leaving a little silence between each chord.)

Practice these exercises also with the same first beat and three chords afterwards in every measure. In other words, in 4/4 time: four quarter notes to the measure.

Now make up some melodies with the right hand while playing the accompaniments you have been practicing. You can also improvise accompaniments to the right hand solo melodies you find in the "Treasure Chest" section of this book.

Right and Left Hand Together.

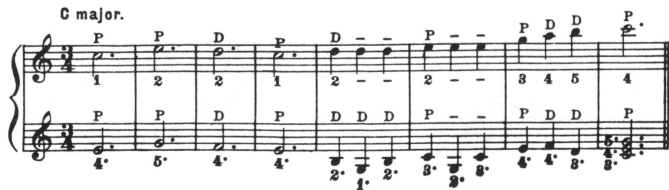

THERE IS A TAVERN IN THE TOWN

There is a tavern in the town, in the town.
And there my true love sits him down, sits him down,
And drinks his wine 'mid laughter gay and free,
and never never thinks of me.

Fare thee well for I must leave thee, Do not
let the parting grieve thee, and re-
member that the best of friends must part, must part.

Adieu, adieu, kind friends, adieu, doo-de-doo.
I can no longer stay with you, stay with you, and I'll
hang my harp on a weeping willow tree, and
may the world go well with thee.

Go to beginning and play
to "Fine".

O SOLE MIO

This classic song introduces a mandolin effect. Adjacent keys are
alternated rapidly when indicated by the sixteenth or thirty-second notes.

How much I love you,
I could never count the ways,
The stars above you
Only surround your face.

And if you leave me
I could never love again.
My heart and soul would
leave with you, my darling.

AMADA MIA, I love you so, you fill my heaven, you fill my soul.
I'll love you -- until you die. And when you leave me, my soul will die.

THE CRUEL WAR IS RAGING

FOLK SONG

THE CRUEL WAR IS RAGING, Johnny has to fight.
I want to be with him, from morning till night.

I'm counting the minutes, hours and the days,
Oh, Lord stop the cruel war.
For this my heart prays.

SWEET ROSIE O'GRADY

Right Hand
plays 8 notes
Higher

Sweet Rosie O'Grady,
My dear little Rose.
She's my steady lady,
Most ev'ryone knows.
And when we are married,
How happy we'll be!
I love sweet Rosie O'Grady,
And Rosie O'Grady loves me.

DOWN BY THE RIVERSIDE

Lyric by
ALBERT GAMSE

Music by
EMANN W. ONKNU

94

FRANKIE AND JOHNNY

Moderato

1. Frank-ie and John-ny were lov-ers, Said they were real-ly in love; Now,
2. Frank-ie and John-ny went walk-ing, John-ny had on_ a new suit; That
3. John-ny said, "I've_ got to leave now, But I won't be_ ver-y long; Don't

Frank-ie was true_ to her John-ny, True as all the stars a-bove; He was her
Frank-ie had bought_ with a "C-note," 'Cause it made him look so cute; He was her
sit up and wait_ for me, hon-ey, Don't you wor-ry while I'm gone;" He was her

man,_____ but he done her wrong.
man,_____ but he done her wrong.
man,_____ but he done her wrong.

4. Frankie went down to the hotel,
   Looked in the window so high,
   There she saw her lovin' Johnny -
   Making love to Nellie Bly,
   He was her man but he done her wrong.

5. Johnny saw Frankie a-comin',
   Down the back stairs he did scott,
   Frankie, she took out her pistol,
   Oh that lady sure could shoot!
   He was her man but he done her wrong.

The Concertina

Diagram showing the notes to be obtained from each key
on **20-keyed** Concertina

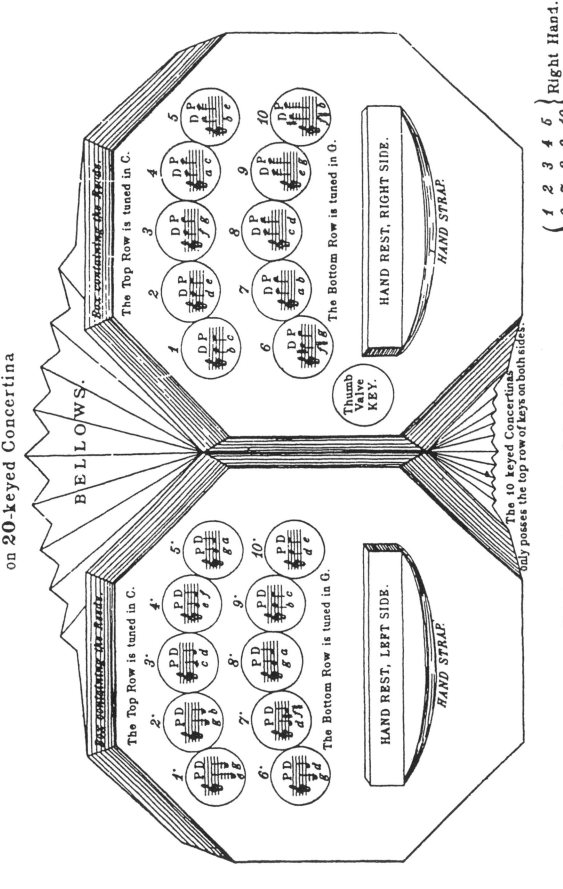

The Top Row is tuned in C.

The Bottom Row is tuned in G.

Box containing the Reeds.

HAND REST, RIGHT SIDE.

HAND STRAP.

Thumb Valve KEY.

HAND REST, LEFT SIDE.

HAND STRAP.

BELLOWS.

The 10 keyed Concertinas only posses the top row of keys on both sides.

Explanation: The letters D and P indicate the action of the bellows. The Keys:
$$\left. \begin{array}{c} 1\ \ 2\ \ 3\ \ 4\ \ 5 \\ 6\ \ 7\ \ 8\ \ 9\ \ 10 \end{array} \right\}\ \text{Right Hand.}$$
$$\left. \begin{array}{c} 1'\ \ 2'\ \ 3'\ \ 4'\ \ 5' \\ 6'\ \ 7'\ \ 8'\ \ 9'\ \ 10' \end{array} \right\}\ \text{Left Hand.}$$
o, g, g, b, or b, o, d, e, etc., the names of the notes.